Three Breaths

Also by nancy brady:

Ohayo Haiku

nancy brady

Three Breaths

Drinian Press/
Huron, Ohio

Three Breaths
Nancy Brady

Copyright © 2013 by Nancy Brady. All rights reserved. Except for use in a review, no part of this book may be reproduced or utilized in any form or by any means electronic or mechanical without permission of the author.

Cover design, photos, and illustrations by Drinian Press LLC

Drinian Press LLC
PO Box 63
Huron, Ohio 44839

Online at www.DrinianPress.com.

Library of Congress Control Number: 2013947843

ISBN-10: 0-9833069-8-2
ISBN-13: 978-0-9833069-8-6

Printed in the United States of America

| Contents |

Three Breaths

Haiku Reduction   1

Haiku   35

Tanka, Haibun, Elfje, Free Verse   55

Acknowledgments   67

For Rob

Haiku Reduction

Haiku Reduction

When I was first introduced to haiku, it was defined as a nature poem tied to a strictly regulated pattern of seventeen syllables broken into three lines of five-seven-five. At the time, this public school definition seemed inviolate and everyone in my small class set to counting syllables on our fingers. When cultural awareness of this Oriental form set in, however, the rules were relaxed. Five-seven-five, as it turned out, meant something different in English than it did in Japanese. The real concept was a poem in one breath which soon translated as three lines, short-long-short. As the form evolved in the Western world, those on the leading edge of the poetry made the argument that a single word could be a haiku. (I don't believe that this newer construction would have ever satisfied the criterion of my high school English teacher, but there it was in a literary journal.) The single word had to then be explained with a paragraph of prose so that the reader could hear a clear poem in a single word.

Haiku reduction is an idea that I have been playing with for a few years. It begins with five-seven-five (or short-long-short) and "reduces" over three repetitions (hence, *three breaths*). It becomes, in a sense, a guided meditation which takes the form of three haiku, each mirroring the others. The final, and shortest form, becomes a single breath which is the heart of haiku.

Nancy Brady												August 2013

A white puffball
explodes across green field
breath scatters seeds

white puffball
explodes in field
scatters seeds

puffball
explodes
seeds

wildflower field…
Queen Anne's lace, blue chicory
mirror sky

wildflowers
lace, blue chicory
mirror sky

wildflower
blue sky

shades of burnished gold
spread upon canvas of green
fall watercolor

shades of gold
spread upon canvas
fall watercolor

gold
canvas
watercolor

the rushing river
slows with the transformation
winter's ice and snow

the river's
transformation
winter ice

ice
transformed
river

white petals on trees
cascading down with the rain
gentle confetti

white petals
cascade with the rain
soft confetti

petals
rain
confetti

snowy white egrets
stalk through river's marshy weeds
avian hunters

snowy egrets
stalk through marsh
hunters

egrets
stalk

milkweed pods open
seeds scatter on the wind
to new life

milkweed pods
seeds on the wind
new life

wind
scatters
life

the soft white feathers
drift slowly down covering
the now silent earth

soft feathers
drift down slowly
silent earth

down
feathers
silence

night skies overhead
an inky blackness dotted
by thousands of stars

night skies
inky blackness dotted
by stars

night
inks
stars

cold and snow
crocus blooms open
hope of spring

cold
spring blooms
crocus

redbud in bloom
purple blossoms peek out
arrival of spring

redbud blooms
blossoms peek out
spring's arrival

redbud
blossoms
arrive

sky washed out by clouds
blues faded to nearly white
color of old jeans

sky-washed clouds
blues faded white
old jeans

washed
blue
jeans

light filters through
dappled leaves of vivid green
shades mossy grass

light through
dappled leaves
shades grass

light
dappled
shades

silhouetted trees
against the gold and mauve sky
while shadows deepen

silhouette trees
gold and mauve sky
shadows deepen

sky
shadows

a lotus flower
drifts lazily on the pond
frog on lily pad

lotus flower
drifts on pond
frog on pad

flower
drifts

pale orb in the sky
burns away wisps of fog
sudden clarity

pale orb
burns away fog
clarity

orb
burns
clear

quiet and pristine
open to the sky above
cathedral of white

quiet
open sky
cathedral

quiet
open
cathedral

red disk in sky
low on the eastern horizon
Japanese flag

red disk
on eastern horizon
Japan's flag

red disk
Japan

splashes of purple
peek out of dark woods
green soon covers

purple splashes
peek from woods
greens soon

woods
peek
green

the water eddies
trees surf down river in
the storm's aftermath

river
eddies
after storm

wings only a blur
flying over a deep pond
two dragonflies mate

wings blur
flying over pond
dragonflies mate

dragonflies
wing

in peaceful lagoon
leaves float on still water
crimson reflections

peaceful lagoon
leaves float on water
still reflections

leaves
float
still

snow on black branches
Canada geese in a Vee
flying of flurries

snow on branches
Canada geese in "V"
flying flurries

snow
geese
flying

tender buds on trees
burst into fragile trees
verdant spring

tender buds
burst into leaves
spring trees

tender
leaves
spring

a mossy garden
reflections in the deep pool
guarded by cattails

mossy garden
deep pool reflections
cattail guard

pool
reflects
cattails

frost covers the ground
fog soft-filters through the trees
night becomes morning

frosted ground
mist through trees
night to give way

frosted
misty
morning

angel in the snow
stands guard and protects
loved ones

snow angel
guards and protects
loved ones

angel
protects
love

tiny buds on tree
burst into delicate blooms
petals of pale pink

buds on trees
burst into bloom
pink petals

trees
bloom

golden sun rises
casting a coppery glow
upon sky, trees, earth

golden sun
casts coppery glow
upon sky, earth

sun
coppery
sky

maples' leaves of gold
flutter down all around
ticker tape parade

golden leaves
flutter down
ticker tape parade

leaves
flutter
parade

pale moon
shines down on two lovers
a warm embrace

moon
shines on lovers'
warm embrace

moon
lovers'
embrace

Grand Teton Mountain
rising above Jackson Hole
where buffalo roam

Grand Teton
rises above Jackson Hole
buffalo roam

Teton
buffalo

Haiku

morning rain
hopscotching around
all the puddles

wind chimes play
in counterpoint to church bells
spring breeze

scarlet-clad
strips away raiment
one leaf at a time

blue jays call
screeching for peanuts
I am well-trained

hummingbird
at scarlet canna lilies
late summer morning

majestic wader
lives on Ohio's north coast
Great Blue heron

wildflower field…
Queen Anne's lace, blue chicory
mirror sky

summer walk
across the fence
blue jays' argument

the computer geeks
play nine holes on the golf course
the real hackers

liquid gold melted
by ice blue water
summer sunset

wings a blur
dragonflies mate
over deep pool

construction barrels
stack cars into single lane
-capillaries

giants' pillow fight--
down blankets
the ground

patriots
the few, the proud, the Marine
fledglings off to war

cornfields
nearly smooth with snow
old man's whiskers

gray winter
amid thorns and brambles
bird in papal red

a dusting of snow
peeping through, purple pansies
still in bloom

snow-covered branches
only color in landscape
cardinal on the bench

white petals
cascade with the rain
soft confetti

spring melancholy
rock 'n rock hits of youth
now classic songs

Cirque Soleil…
the squirrels' acrobatics
on the feeder

March blizzard
red-winged blackbirds
flock to feeder

late snowfall
after the ice cream stand opens
spring ala mode

red disk in sky
low on the eastern horizon
Japanese flag

cherry blossoms
drift down into the lake
the white swans

Morse code signals
through the dark woods
farmhouse lights

crabgrass claws
grab ankles on sidewalk
late summer

turned to gold
the silver aspens'
alchemy

imperious gaze
from wire perch
red-tailed hawk

shades of red
on canvas of green
fall palette

crimson trees
amid boughs of green
a first kiss

powdered sugar
tops freshly plowed field
late fall morning

Japanese maples
their leaves a fiery red
against ice blue sky

late summer
two leaves drift down
to the ground

summer storm
hosta leaves shelter
a rabbit

upon the old stump
bracket fungi multiplies
from decay, new life

dead of night
the long whooo whooo
of the train through town

Canada geese call
urge sluggish wings to flight
late summer morning

placebo effect…
Vicodin now in hand
patient's face changes to smile

African violets
in bloom on Grandma's birthday
summer solstice

Queen Anne's lace
remembrance of Grandma's
rhinestone brooch

irritated by a cell phone ring
only to discover
it is mine

gnarled tree trunk
my mother's
arthritic hands

dime on the sidewalk
a gentle reminder
to tithe

pecking order...
competition to be
mom's favorite

loss of family members
addition of new ones
lateral buds

pumpkin pie
still my favorite
birthday cake

heat lightning
lights up evening sky
teen's tantrum

Solar collector—the cat stretches her full-length on the couch, catching the noonday sun, moving
as the sun moves

the soft purr that rumbles and warms me through to my core

winter's chill
wrapping hands around a warm cuppa
and the cat's purr

hunkered down on porch
eight cats and kittens
bask in the morning sun

cat as familiar
warmth, comfort of soft purr
close by

paw prints in snow…a feral cat to the stream of water

Tanka

Haibun

Elfje

Free Verse

lapful of cat
soaks in sun's warmth
through windows

I, too, am warmer
from the sun and cat's purr

the grass becomes green
yet, sprinkled between blades
violets of blue

I know they don't belong
but still bring a smile

Summer Sail

When motoring out the river to sail on Lake Erie, we pass the local limestone plant and note the smoke stacks for the wind direction. The limestone is brought to the riverbank via large tankers that cruise the waters of the Great Lake, and then is piled up alongside the break wall.

Gazing northward towards Ontario are the Great Blue herons. Flexing their wings like giant bats, black cormorants sit upon pilings that sit above the river's water line while the snowy egrets fly over to the other side of the river to the shallow, sheltered bay to fish. Various species of ducks glide alongside our boat, but the largest flock of birds are the ring-billed and herring gulls. All the while the great mountains of limestone play host to hundreds of gulls and terns. Screeching loudly, they sun themselves as we put up our mainsail on the way out of the river for a day of sail.

> King of the mountain
> A game played by seagulls
> On the rock piles

Green
Fluttering fans
Tended by monks
Has it slipped memory?
Gingko

Dusty
Chalk marks
On the sidewalk
I toss a pebble
Hopscotch

White
Floats down
Drifts across sidewalk
Grass covered in snow?
Cottonwood

Jackhammer
Drills deeply
Hearing the rat-a-tat-tat
Did he find insects?
Woodpecker

Return to earth

Reduce, recycle, reuse,
the bird, not celebrated,
  (except in Hinckley)
follows the premise.

Gliding, winging its way
Clearing
fields and highways--
each spring
returning
to winter's detritus.

The reaper's shadow
  watches for death,
gliding and soaring on thermals,
joined now by companions.

Hulking Skeksis
  tearing at decaying flesh,
  ripping from bones.

Without status
  of raptor hawk
Scavengers
feast on leftovers.
Reduce,
recycle,
reuse.

Dictionary Elles

Lewd, lascivious, licentious, lustful, libertine…
  Who discovered them?
  Was it Christy?
  Karen?
  Or, perhaps, another?
No matter, we learned them
Different words with subtle nuances
All with the same meaning.

We knew them, used them
We were the Dictionary Girls
  Virgins all,
Dateless on Saturday nights.

We believed our teachers,
  The ones who said,
"If you use a word ten times,
The word is yours forever."

And we made them ours,
Lewd, lascivious, licentious, lustful, libertine.
It became our mantra; each having her favorite

Mine, licentious…
   I loved the sound, the feeling of it in my mouth
   Feline, lithe, lean, and smoldering,
   A svelte woman in a skinny black dress.

We're grown now,
   Having lived the lustful life of the mind
   Still Dictionary Girls
…and have become, in turn,
Lewd, lascivious, licentious, lustful libertines
   At times.
 but mostly we are just
   Dictionary Girls.

Come September

The sky's blue enough
to rival
  a jay's
  wing.

Trees greening
  in the last
  hurrah of
chlorophyll
Not yet eclipsed
  by crimson, scarlet,
    and gold.

Burgundy spears
  of sumac,
point in defiance,
not relinquishing
color

More vibrant now,
  the colors imprint on
  the mind,
  to stave off
  winter's grays,
so
come, September.

Golden fans

Carpets of golden fans
from four ginkgo trees.
I see them
    on my walks
        around town.

A giant at the park
  overlooking the lake,
    another in front of the library,
      at a church, and
        again, on the path from here to there.
Each leaving a carpet of fans behind.

The orphan offspring of monks,
the oldest of trees.
Male and female, they come
bearing the 'fruit' that helps
with memory.

Is that why they are planted?
To keep in memory those
who are gone?
With plaques to recall
  when memory dims?

Living for thousands of years,
  the trees will outlast the
people, the memories.
The golden fans will cover the rest.

Acknowledgments:

Dusty chalk marks (elfje) was first published on May 7, 2012 at www.simplyelfje.wordpress.com

Green fluttering fans (elfje) was first published on May 25, 2012 at www.simplyelfje.wordpress.com

Crimson trees (haiku) was first published on January 19, 2008 at www.asahi.com

Morning rain (haiku) was first published on April 29, 2011 at www.asashi.com

Loss of family members (haiku) was first published on March 16, 2012 at www.asahi.com

Solar collector (small stone) was first published in the anthology *pay attention: a river of stones* edited by Fiona Robyn and Kaspalita, (Lulu.com) April 14, 2011

Other poems have appeared online at:
        www.redroom.com/nancysmith

www.ingramcontent.com/pod-product-compliance
Lightning Source LLC
Chambersburg PA
CBHW051714040426
42446CB00008B/879